DEFINING MOMENTS

Growing to Know, Love, and Serve the Lord

DICK WALSMAN

WESTBOW
PRESS®
A DIVISION OF THOMAS NELSON
& ZONDERVAN

WestBow Press books may be ordered through booksellers or by contacting:

WestBow Press
A Division of Thomas Nelson & Zondervan
1663 Liberty Drive
Bloomington, IN 47403
www.westbowpress.com
844-714-3454

ISBN: 978-1-6642-8401-2 (sc)
ISBN: 978-1-6642-8403-6 (hc)
ISBN: 978-1-6642-8402-9 (e)

Library of Congress Control Number: 2022921227

Print information available on the last page.

WestBow Press rev. date: 12/28/2022

WHAT PEOPLE ARE SAYING ABOUT
DEFINING MOMENTS

For decades I have known Dick Walsman as a true disciple of Jesus Christ—a lifelong learner and follower of Jesus Christ, and a man passionate about evangelism and making disciples. Weaving together his authentic story and biblical passages and principles, *Defining Moments* will help you grow in experiencing the vibrant life of knowing, loving, and serving Jesus.

Mark Slaughter: Evangelist & Director of Evangelistic Partners; InterVarsity Christian Fellowship/USA; Board member, Leighton Ford Ministries

I learned some time ago that personal stories are the best way to communicate a truth. This book is the personal story of a man who has walked with God many years and found him to be faithful. There is so much truth contained about living the Christ-centered life that you will find this book to be very helpful, useful, encouraging, and practical. I am delighted to endorse and recommend *Defining Moments* whole heartedly.

Ron Blue: CEO, Ron Blue Institute

"God knows when to reach us at just the right time. Dick Walsman talks about his walk with Christ in *Defining Moments; Growing to Know, Love and Serve the Lord.* It was God's providence that his wife Ginny connected with a former missionary who helped them better understand the Bible. She, and then Dick, accepted Jesus as their Savior. He shares his journey - and the things he learned along the way in this fascinating book."

Governor Scott Walker: President, Young America's Foundation Formerly Wisconsin Governor

All believers can relate to trusting God when life doesn't make sense. Dick takes this struggle head on. He shares his life-earned wisdom to guide the reader through the process of having confidence in God no matter what life throws at you. Readers will be encouraged, convicted, and challenged in their faith after reading "*Defining Moments.*" Dick navigates with all how to walk in the fullness of life that Christ offers.

Erik Daniels: Executive V. P., Ronald Blue Trust

The typical prison inmate that reads this book will learn so much about God and His grace. They admit that they didn't live a perfect life, so how could God forgive them? The quote of Jerry Bridges in chapter 4 should give them hope.

"Your worst days are never so bad that you are beyond the reach of God's grace, and your best days are never so good that you are beyond the need of God's grace."

Jimmy Cochran: Director of Team Operations, Saints Prison Ministry

Defining Moments is an inspiring and insightful life journey with God. Our sovereign and loving God often brings life-changing revelation across our path through unusual circumstances. This helps us discover the purpose for our life. The book chronicles the pivotal biblical truths that will help transform any life for eternal significance. Take time to reflect.

Helmut Teichert: Executive Director, Henry Brandt Ministries

I have had the extreme joy of knowing Dick Walsman for the last four years. He is a man of vast biblical knowledge and integrity. I have observed him personally as he has labored to write his new book, *Defining Moments: Growing to Know, Love, and Serve the Lord.* His heart's desire is that this book would serve as a springboard for those desiring to live out Christianity in their daily lives.

In *Defining Moments*, readers will find beautiful stories of Dick's life experiences wrapped around scripture that will encourage them in their personal walks with Jesus. It is with my most enthusiastic recommendation and greatest respect that I recommend *Defining Moments* to you—for personal growth, reflection and encouragement.

Dr. Jeremy Morton: Lead Pastor, First Baptist Church, Woodstock, GA

What an ironic honor that my friend, Dick Walsman, would ask me to endorse his book, *Defining Moments: Growing to Know, Love and Serve the Lord*. Ironic, because the single most defining moment in my own life occurred in their home fifty-five years ago at a neighborhood Bible club. It was through the simple yet powerful teaching of Dick's wife, Ginny, that I first heard, understood, and trusted in the Gospel of Jesus Christ.

While I am eternally grateful for that first encounter with Dick and Ginny, they have been part of several other defining moments in my life through the years. Moments like that are what Dick lives for, so don't be surprised if reading this profound story of God's faithful work in his life turns out to be one of your defining moments.

Phil Tuttle: President and CEO, Walk Thru the Bible ministry

Dedicated to my wife, Ginny Walsman.

For the most part, we are like most husbands and wives, but there are many special things about her. She trusted in Christ as Savior some months before me. She grew, but I didn't. One of our children was asked by a friend one day if her parents ever quarreled. She responded, "Not that I know of, except over religion."

Ginny never shamed me, but little by little, she bought me Christian books. I wasn't quick to start reading them, but eventually I wanted answers to spiritual questions. The more I learned, the more I wanted to learn.

Bottom line: I owe much to her for the Christian life I have enjoyed for over fifty years. And she has trusted me with her life in many ways.

CONTENTS

FOREWORD

Dick Walsman has been a dear brother and friend whom I have admired for several decades. Over that time, I've observed him grow into a committed churchman, a mature elder statesman, and a patriarch of the Christian faith.

In *Defining Moments* Dick unpacks his unique life and walk with Jesus. And he does this by relating details of his spiritual journey as seen through the crucial biblical progression of *"Knowing God, Loving God and Serving God."* And this adventure is illustrated throughout by pertinent Bible passages and that have shaped his life and thus saturate the book. We should all be so thoughtful, conscientious and deliberate as we thoroughly think through the eternal consequences and lasting legacies of our own lives.

John Isch, MD: Retired heart surgeon; Board Chair, Walk Thru the Bible ministry

PREFACE

We all have times in our lives that can be considered defining moments. We may not know when or what they will be, but significant things happen that change our lives—not for just a moment but forever.

We weren't considering anything associated with God when my wife, Ginny, and I were invited to attend an event with lectures on the book *Communism versus Freedom* taught by an ex-Christian missionary, Tim Warner. I thought, *What does a missionary know about that?*

To our surprise, he told us more than expected when he brought up the matter of faith in God and defending the Bible as being true. He pointed out that communism is a system that isn't embraced by everyone and doesn't include God. Tim rebutted that assessment with his position that belief in God contained the true answer for life, which is where he had placed his faith.

Addressing his short, confident statement, Ginny asked Tim for help in learning about the Bible. It didn't take long until we joined a group. I had my doubts but agreed to join the group anyway. That sequence of events led us to attend a church that not only talked about the Christian life, but their people lived by

Christian values in a relationship with God. Eventually, I learned enough to accept Jesus Christ as my Savior, which Ginny had already done some months before, all because a friend invited us to attend some lectures.

Defining Moments

The title of this book is *Defining Moments*. A moment is a specific point or series of connected events when something significant happens that has an eternal impact on a life.

Looking back, consider all that happened associated with our attending the event.

- An impressive, knowable ex-missionary gave lectures on communism and talked about his faith in God.
- He defended the Bible.
- Ginny wanted to learn from the Bible.
- Being a part of the Bible study group convinced us that the Bible was true.
- A Bible-believing, loving church nurtured our inquiring minds.

Skeptics may say that all of these were just by chance. I consider them all pieces of a puzzle that, when fit together, lead us to faith in Jesus Christ.

Defining moments can be something big, happening all at once, or a process of smaller events leading to a conclusion. Ginny and I could have been called "seekers," who are open but not yet ready to believe. God knew it, but He didn't push us. He knew when we were ready—Ginny first and me a couple of months later. I remember the time but not the date when I admitted to myself that I was through vacillating; either believe or I reject it all. To the best of my knowledge, that is when I became a true

Christian with a relationship with Jesus Christ, what some might call "born again."

That decision defined the rest of my life. I would not be a passive Christian just warming a church pew. I would be a genuine follower of Christ. However, as a child of God, I had much to learn about how to live the life.

Thank God Ginny was eager to see me grow, so she started buying books related to the Bible. As I saw how practical the Bible was, I started buying books dealing with many life issues. I didn't just read to be reading; I read to study. I began outlining books and then set up files to keep the articles and notes I had saved. I read to learn from some of the best Christian authors. Now I can hardly believe how far I have come.

As I was planning to write a book, I needed a title, something catchy like *Defining Moments,* but then I wanted to draw people to seek a vital relationship with the Lord so I added *Growing to Know, Love, and Serve the Lord* as a subtitle. After all, those were the moments that impacted my life.

I was motivated to write this book because it seemed like many Christians were missing the fullness in life that Christ offers. It wasn't enough to just be saved for me; I wanted more out of my relationship with Jesus. I have been blessed and strengthened in my faith by the awesome example of dedicated believers. It is not necessarily just facts a person wants; we need the Bible to impact our lives, connecting the personal with facts. I wrap my personal stories around facts in some of my defining moments.

At the time, I was still thinking about what to include in the book. I read a newsletter from Ken Ham, founder of the famous Creation Museum and Ark Encounter. He was very concerned that churches were hardly teaching anything about creation, and evolution was taking hold of more and more minds. He compared the Bible's creation account to that of evolution and couldn't imagine that people would believe evolution theories.

That was when I decided that the book's first chapter would concern creation. I am so glad because what I learned from my studies of both issues strengthened my faith like never before. Building on creation, I personally needed to build a picture of the character of God (chapter 2). In chapter 3, I talk about how we can know Him through the Holy Spirit as He inspired the writing of the Bible and lives within us.

The other ten chapters deal with life as a Christian and have personally impacted my faith. It's a process to grow in trusting and obeying God, abiding in Christ, peace, faith, hope, love, etc.

It's my hope that as you read this book, you begin to think through your own defining moments, events in your life that have determined your relationship with God. I hope you come to believe that *if this worked for Dick, it'll work for me.*

Chapter 1

GOD IN CREATION

What we believe about creation can—no, *will*—make a huge difference both here and now and for eternity. Some may think it's a choice between equals and it really doesn't matter what is decided, but it isn't. Moreover, it will be the most significant decision a person will ever make because death will one day come to everyone.

Nothing existed before God created the universe. Evolution, however, theorizes that Earth was formed by particles from a vast explosion, either from an explosion of a planet or a tremendous growth of inanimate particles drifting in the universe coming together.

With both creation and evolution, proof positive of either

1

option isn't available. Both must be accepted by faith because there were no witnesses to observe what took place. God used what would be called "miracles." Evolution contends that combining chance, time, and natural selection took millions of years to evolve.

On the surface, God's creation seems to be the most logical conclusion because it happened all at once. However, the teaching of godless evolution has become center stage. Evolution can be taught to our children in schools, but the Bible cannot.

Charles Darwin is the best-known evolutionist. I understand that he once had religious leanings but rejected the notion of God. He and others sought answers for creation apart from a higher power.

God gave us the capacity to reason, and He expects it to be used. Therefore, my faith isn't just a blind leap of faith but based on reasonable conclusions. The better we come to know God as He really is, the more we will come to love and serve Him.

God in Creation

The Bible opens in Genesis, revealing God's actions in creation. Imagine how much of God's message would be missed if the Bible just said, "God created." The detail is essential, especially in comparison to evolution.

Naturally, we can wonder why God created the world and everything in it. William Barclay gives his opinion in The Daily Study Bible series.

> Why did God create a world where there would be so much strife among humans, a world that would bring Him so much grief? The answer is that creation was essential to His very nature. If God is love, He cannot

exist in lonely isolation. Love must have someone to love and someone to love it.[1]

This gives a reason for why God created the universe, but what about how it happened?

The Genesis Account

God obviously intended for Earth to be populated with living beings, creatures, and plant life. There had to be an environment necessary for life to exist. So far as we know, the rest of the universe will not sustain life.

Ric Ergenbright captured the creative mind of God in his awesome pictorial book, *The Art of God: Heavens and the Earth*.[2] In it, he points out four essential elements required for life on planet Earth.

Air: Air is essential for physical life. Without oxygen, we would die quickly. That's why astronauts could not survive without spacesuits. Earth is unique in the universe.

Water: It is the most basic and vital element of humans and nature. So far, water has not been seen on any planet we know.

Fire: Without heat rays and the temperature of the sun, our Earth would be uninhabitable.

---

[1] William Barclay, *The Daily Bible Series* (Philadelphia, PA: The Westminster Press)

[2] Ric Ergenbright, *The Art of God: Heavens and the Earth* (Wheaton, IL: Tyndale House Publishers, 1999) 19–35

Earth: How could we grow crops to eat, raise animals, and have important minerals? The initial makeup of Earth was inanimate material.

Of God's heavens, King David wrote in the book of Psalms in majestic terms.

> The heavens declare the glory of God: the skies proclaim the work of his hands. Day after day, they pour forth speech: night after night, they display his knowledge. (Psalm 19:1–2)

Days, Times, and Mountains

Some people reject the notion that God could speak things into existence in twenty-four-hour periods. Jesus said, "With God, nothing is impossible" (Luke 1:37). God demonstrated His power through the miracles performed by Jesus Christ.

In Christ, God restored sight to a blind man from birth. To an invalid of thirty-eight years, not able to walk, Jesus said, "Pick up your mat and walk," and made him well (John 5:1–15). Jesus rebuked the winds from a furious squall by saying, "Quiet! Be still." And the winds died down (Mark 4:35–41).

Did He have to make quick decisions about what He would do from one day to the next? If you consider eternal time, God had plenty of time to plan what He would do. He was ready in a moment to speak life into existence. J. I. Packer once commented that what God planned in eternity, He carried out in time.

Here's a summarization of the Bible's six days of God's work in creation:

First: Light and darkness were formed, making day and night.

Second: Waters were separated from the land.

Third: Dry ground appeared. Now there were land and seas. The land would produce vegetation: seed-bearing plants and trees, according to their *kinds*.

Fourth: Days were established to mark seasons and years. The greater light (sun) governs the day, and the lesser light (moon) governs the night. Work in the light; sleep in the dark.

Fifth: Water would teem with living creatures, and birds would fly above Earth. According to their *kind*, they were to be fruitful and increase in number.

Sixth: Land produced living creatures according to their kinds: livestock, creatures that move along the ground, and wild animals, each according to its *kind*. Not ending His creative work, God created male and female in the image of God.

God saw all that He had made, and it was not only good but "very good." It was all by God's design.

According to Their Kind

There is a vast difference in evolutionary theories compared to God's creation account. God spoke things into existence in a few days, while evolution says they took hundreds of millions of years to evolve.

The answer for the *variation* in species ("kinds") is difficult to explain in evolution, which is based on long periods of chance, time, and "random selection."

In Genesis 1:11–24, God addresses "kinds" ten times. In verse 11, He states,

> Let the land produce vegetation: seed-bearing plants and trees on the land that bear fruit with seed in it, according to their various kinds.

Not only were there kinds (species) of seed-bearing plants and trees, but there were also birds, fish, livestock, and wild animals according to their kinds.

Dogs would be dogs. A kind does not mean that every dog would be the same color or breed. In Genesis 1:11, God created "according" to their various kinds. So among the species of dogs, there can be poodles, cocker spaniels, and bulldogs. They could mate together. However, a dog cannot mate with a pig.

My point is that random acts would not create specific categories or kinds, but design would.

Be Fruitful and Multiply

If I were to challenge evolution's well-established position concerning creation, it wouldn't be a complex subject like the complexity of eyeballs. Subjects like that can be disputed. I would pick something more obvious. The most obvious to me is the existence of the male and female sexes and reproduction.

Evolution lacks important answers concerning the issue of sex and reproduction. What are the chances that male and female bodies could become so much the same yet different?

If everything were created by chance, what accounts for the

unique differences in anatomy, especially sexual anatomy? Across the whole spectrum of humans, animals, and even plants, there are unique differences, depending on their kind. Did this happen by chance or by design?

Basically, except for sexual anatomy differences, male and female bodies are essentially the same. God designed it so that the male and female could be joined. But joining couldn't have been possible if it were not for the male's nervous and vascular systems. The nervous system responded to stimulation, sending blood to the male's private part.

During "laying together" (a Bible term), the male passes sperm into the female. Her body, usually at the same time each month, creates eggs. If things go well, the sperm and egg join to conceive an eventual offspring.

Once conception takes place, the different design of the shape of the female womb provides an adequate place for the fetus to develop. When it's time for delivery, the flexible pelvis shifts to provide enough space for the child's head to pass.

In the womb, the fetus is provided nourishment. Once born, the child continues to need liquid to survive. Uniquely, the mother's breasts offer milk from which the baby is nourished. Newborn babies have the instinct to suck.

Draw your own conclusion. Was it chance or design?

Choices

Without a higher power, it might be a toss-up between evolution and creation. I might choose evolution. After all, the other choice is based on miracles.

Even though evolution involves chance, time, and natural selection, things might well have happened as the theories provide, but those could also be considered miracles.

Nevertheless, evolution deals with the past, and it ends there. We just live, and then we die. There aren't any books involving evolution that say anything about how to live our lives or what comes after our lives.

Chapter 2

THE FAMILY OF GOD

But when the time had fully come, God
sent his son, born of a woman,
born under the law, to redeem those under the law,
that we might have the full right of sons.
Because you are sons, God sent the
Spirit of his Son into our hearts,
the Spirit who calls out, "Abba, Father."
So you are no longer a slave, but a son;
and you are a son, and since you are a son,
God has made you also an heir.
—Galatians 4:4–7

Some think that using the phrase "Abba, Father" is like calling God "Daddy," but a more correct meaning conveys the idea of the authority, warmth, and intimacy of a loving father's care (see Matthew 6:9 ESV). Only Jesus and Paul of all the apostles used the term Father to indicate a strong personal relationship with Him.

Dick Walsman

Old Testament Father

To many, the Old Testament God was considered mongering and judgmental, but what would any of us have thought if we were faced with a hostile environment, both the rebellious nation of Israel and war-mongering foes? The Israelites were given guidance but often refused it and suffered from disobedience. God had to use extreme measures to deal with their disobedience to His commands, even though the commands were meant for their good.

Moses knew the heart of God was for their own good, and he said to the people,

> Keep his decrees and commands, which I am giving you today, so that it may go well with you and your children after you and that you may live long in the land the Lord your God gives you for all time. (Deuteronomy 4:40)

God's point all along was to love and protect the Israelites.

But then there was me, flat on my face in a hotel room, feeling unworthy of myself. I was just not measuring up in life as much as I should be. I picked up the Bible in the room and turned to the psalms with short verses and many expressions of God's love. I just happened to start reading Psalm 103.

The more I read, the better I started to feel about myself. God felt good about me despite my sins. To this day, there are verses highlighted.

> Praise the Lord, O my soul; all my inmost being, praise his holy name. Praise the Lord, O my soul, and forget not all his benefits—who forgives all your sin and heals all your diseases. (Psalm 103:1–3)

The Lord is compassionate and gracious, slow to anger, abounding in love. (Psalm 103:8)

As a father has compassion on his children, so the Lord has compassion on those who fear (respect) him; for he knows how we are formed, he remembers that we are dust. (Psalm 103:13–14)

Even though we don't compare to God's greatness in creation, we are this important to Him:

For God so loved the world that he gave his one and only Son, that whoever believes in him shall not perish but have eternal life. (John 3:16)

New Testament Father

Instead of dealing with a rebellious *nation,* God, through Jesus Christ as a human, became deeply involved with *individuals.* Only once in the Old Testament was God referred to as "Father"—the father of the Jewish nation. In the New Testament, God is often referred to as "Father," which sounds more intimate than God.

As humans, we consider God a spirit, so we can never see Him. Through Jesus, God became flesh and lived among the people to show what He was like. Jesus was sinless. I love this saying: "He became as I am so that I could become as He is."

God did not change, but our perception of Him became different. The New Testament brought something new and significant in that believers become children of God, part of the family of God. Even adopted, a child has the same rights and privileges as a biological child.

Days before Jesus would face His death on the cross, Philip asked Jesus to show him the Father.

> Jesus answered: "Don't you know me, Philip; even after I have been among you such a long time? Anyone who has seen Me has seen the Father. How can you say, 'Show us the Father?' Don't you believe that I am in the Father, and that the Father is in me? The words I say to you are not just my own. Rather, it is the Father, living in Me, who is doing the work. Believe Me when I say that I am in the Father and the Father is in Me." (John 14:9–11)

God became Jesus with skin on.

Knowing God as Father

Imagine the following dialogue between a soon-to-be adopted orphan and God's Word.

What will it be like with a new father? Even though You know my past, please reveal Yourself to me in ways that say, "I love you, My new child."

> But God demonstrates His own love for us in this: While we were still sinners, Christ died for us. (Romans 5:8)

I couldn't trust my birth father; will it be any different with You?

> Trust in the Lord with all your heart and lean not on your own understanding; in all your ways acknowledge Him, and He will make your way straight. (Proverbs 3:5–6)

Will You be with me for the long haul or someday reject me?

Never will I leave you: never will I forsake you. (Hebrews 13:5)

I expect that You will treat me nicely to begin with, but will Your love for me last?

For I am convinced that neither death nor life, neither angels nor demons, neither the present nor the future, nor any powers, neither height nor depth, nor anything else in all creation, will be able to separate us from the love of God that is in Christ Jesus our Lord. (Romans 8:38–39)

Child of God

The apostle John knew Jesus as well as any other apostle. He understood that Jesus, the Son of God, spoke for the Father. There was an intimate "family" relationship between them which the Father was eager to have with anyone who would believe in Jesus.

The Holy Spirit, through John, said,

Yet to all who received him (Jesus), to those who believed in his name, he gave the right to become children of God—children born of not of natural descent, nor of human decision or a husband's will, but born of God. (John 1:12–13)

At His miraculous virgin birth, God was given the name Jesus, which means Emmanuel, which means "God is with us."

Sometimes our human father gave commands, but often they were merely instructions. They weren't meant to be orders like "Do it or else" but dealt with things that would be good for the family.

The apostle John frequently referred to God's children in 1 John. That book is one of my most loved books of the Bible. The word "children" appears more times in that book than any other, from the book of Acts to 3 John.

> Dear friends, now we are *children* of God, and what we will be has not yet been made known. But we know that when he appears, we shall be like him, for we shall see him as he is. Everyone who has this hope in him purifies himself, just as he is pure. (1 John 3:2)

> Jesus Christ laid down his life for us. And we ought to lay down our lives for our brothers. Dear *children*, let us not love with words or tongue but with actions and in truth. (1 John 3:18)

> And now, dear *children*, continue in him, so that when he appears we may be confident and unashamed before him at his coming. (1 John 2:28)

> How great is the love the Father has lavished on us that we should be called *children* of God! And that is what we are! (1 John 3:1)

> Jesus Christ laid down his life for us. And we ought to lay down our lives for our brothers. Dear *children*, let us not love with words or tongue but with actions and in truth. (1 John 3:18)

As children, we focus on our needs and getting them met. But as we mature, we become aware of our father and mother, who they are, and what they do. Our relationship changes over time as our relationship grows deeper and deeper.

Chapter 3

HOLY SPIRIT: GOD'S GIFT TO BELIEVERS

So from now on, we regard no one
from a worldly point of view.
Though we once regarded Christ in
this way, we do so no longer.
Therefore, if anyone is in Christ,
he is a new creation;
the old has gone, the new has come.
—2 Corinthians 5:16–17

I don't remember ever hearing anything about the Holy Spirit when I was growing up. If I did ever hear the word *spirit,* I would think of some invisible thing drifting around, doing whatever things spirits do. Where does the Holy Spirit fit into Christianity?

I Want More than Religion; I Want a Relationship

Accepting Jesus Christ as my Savior was new to me when I was thirty-two years old. Before then, He was just a person in history teaching and showing compassion. Now His Spirit would be in me, and I would be like the early disciples when Jesus told them He would leave to go to His Father in heaven.

Preparing His disciples for the future, Jesus told them what to expect in His absence. The Counselor, the Holy Spirit, would replace him.

> But when he, the Holy Spirit of truth, comes, he will guide you into all truth. He will not speak on his own; he will speak only what he hears, and he will tell you what is to come.
>
> He will bring glory to me (Christ) by taking from what is mine and making it known to you. All that belongs to the Father is mine. That is why I said the Spirit will take from what is mine and make it known to you. (John 16:13–14)

The Holy Spirit is a Person, not an impersonal *force* such as electricity. My failures can grieve him, yet He fills me with love, joy, and peace. Unlike in the Old Testament, when the Spirit came only on special occasions, in the New Testament, He came to indwell believers *forever*.

It is the Spirit who gives Jesus the ability to be everywhere and with everyone at the same time. Before, Jesus was limited to time and space, but now He will be present at any time and place. The Bible says He will never leave us or forsake us.

Beginnings

I trace the history of coming to know and live by the Holy Spirit starting when Ginny and I were pleased to have two Campus Crusade for Christ (Cru) staff members spend a couple of nights with us. They would visit students at the local university. After spending the first day and the night with students, they couldn't wait to share their experiences with us.

The whole time they were with us, they were so enthusiastic. As relatively new believers, we had never heard Christians be so joyful about sharing Jesus Christ with others. Wanting to learn how to share Christ with others, they urged us to attend a conference that weekend sponsored by Cru.

Harry, the event leader, impressed me when I learned that He had given up his business interest to join Cru. As the event ended, he invited Ginny and me to attend an executive seminar at Cru's California headquarters. Attendees would mostly be people of accomplishment and influence.

Should we go? I knew more progress was needed in my new life in Christ. I also was curious about successful people who were Christians. *If it worked for them, hopefully, it would work for me.* So we lined up a babysitter and went to southern California.

Impressed with Harry, I was also impressed that some of the breakout sessions were taught by laypeople. With our limited knowledge of the Bible, we decided to attend a session on the Holy Spirit.

This would be the first time we learned anything about the Holy Spirit. What we were *taught* and what we *caught* from the impressive examples of others would make a huge difference in our lives.

It is interesting looking back. Two enthusiastic Cru staff members urged us to attend Harry's training event. He encouraged us to attend the executive seminar, where we were introduced to teaching about the Holy Spirit. What a "defining moment" it became!

There is much more to know about the Holy Spirit than I cover here, but what I cover is foundational. *The Transforming Power of the Gospel,* written by Jerry Bridges, helped me in my growth.

Being Filled with the Spirit

The subject of the Holy Spirit can be complex. The speaker at the Cru conference was able only to break the ice on the subject. Seeking more spiritual growth, what I learned was enough to pursue more understanding about the Holy Spirit.

It didn't take long after returning home to find out that various denominations said little or nothing about the Holy Spirit. Some were more emotional than others when addressing the Spirit. It sounded like the Holy Spirit was important in living my faith, and I needed to get reasonable answers.

I learned more about the Holy Spirit from Dr. Bill Bright, president of Cru, and Dr. Henry Brandt, a biblically based Christian counselor. I use the term "biblically based" because the Bible supported everything I learned from them. Materials written by Dr. Bright have influenced parts of what I have written.

I wasn't as interested in the theology of the Holy Spirit as I was in *how* the Holy Spirit would change my life. As He works to bring about change, it's referred to as the "ministry of the Holy Spirit." Probably the most known aspect is called the "fruit of the Spirit."

> But the fruit of the Spirit is love, joy, peace, patience, kindness, goodness, faithfulness, gentleness, and self-control. (Galatians 5:22–23)

And we pray this in order that you may live a life worthy of the Lord and may please Him in every way: bearing fruit in every good work, growing in the knowledge of God, being strengthened with all *power* according to His glorious might so that you may have great endurance, etc. (Colossians 1:10–11)

Power

Speaking for myself, I knew I failed in many respects for these characteristics to be evident. Without the Holy Spirit in my life, before I received Christ, it was all about my way. If people didn't like what I did or said, that was their problem.

After becoming born again, some things immediately changed. However, I struggled with others. Maybe I needed a greater presence of the Spirit. I hadn't yet learned that I had to yield more of myself to the Spirit. He needed to be able to fill me so that He could be in charge.

Therefore, do not be foolish but understand what the Lord's will is. Do not get drunk on wine, which leads to debauchery. Instead, *be filled with the Spirit*. Speak to one another with psalms, hymns, and spiritual songs. Sing and make music in your heart to the Lord, always giving thanks to God the Father for everything, in the name of our Lord Jesus Christ. (Ephesians 5:17–20)

Paul had concerns that the Ephesians live wisely and understand and live according to God's will. The world around them had no interest in such things. Rather than getting drunk in riotous living, they should be doing things associated with godly fellowship and living, things that would bring thanks to God for everything.

Paul's statement to "be filled with the Spirit" was not just a suggestion but a command meant for every Christian. To "be filled" means that God's power is so in control of a person that they can do what God wishes. It is then up to a person to yield themselves to the work of the Holy Spirit.

Jesus said He came so that we may have a fulfilled life (John 10:10). The issue is who is in charge. Who knows better what God's will is? The Holy Spirit works to carry out God's will. When temptations come our way, we need to realize that the devil tempts us to get the worst out of us while God wants the best for us.

To be filled is not just a one-and-done matter. The Greek word for *being filled* conveys the idea of "be being filled." In other words, it means that we should practice living continually under the control of the Holy Spirit.

Sin separates us from the power of God. As mentioned elsewhere, if we know we have sinned, we should confess the moment we sin.

Being filled is not necessarily an emotional experience. Instead, it refers to the attitudes and actions that come from a believer. In writing to the Galatians, Paul said,

> So I say, live by the Spirit, and you will not gratify the desires of the sinful nature … Since we live by the Spirit, let us keep in step with the Spirit. (Galatians 5:16, 25)

Receiving Christ for salvation is easy from the standpoint that it is an act of faith, trusting Jesus for our forgiveness, which can be done in a moment. However, once we have been saved, there is the aspect of living in obedience to His ways and will.

There are times when I could, or should, do something that

I knew would be the wish of Christ. But then again, there are things I did that I knew I shouldn't have done. Things could have been different if I had been filled with the Spirit.

> For the sinful nature desires what is contrary to the Spirit, and the Spirit what is contrary to the sinful nature. They are in conflict with each other. They are in conflict with each other, so that you do not do what you want. (Galatians 5:17)

According to the Greek meaning of "be filled," it conveys the ideas of power and control. To me, power is like *motivation*. If I don't have the motivation, the Spirit will provide it.

Challenges and opportunities are part of our lives. At times I haven't been motivated to do something. Because of fear of failure or timidity, opportunities to serve were passed.

> For God did not give us a spirit of timidity, but a spirit of power, of love, and of self-discipline. (2 Timothy 1:7)

It's like two Alaskan sled dogs fighting with each other. Someone asks, "Which one wins most times." Answer: "The one I feed the most." Food is power to the dog, just as the power of the Holy Spirit motivates to be and do the will of God.

Control

The last "fruit of the Spirit," self-control, concerns self-discipline. It sounds like I have a responsibility to live like a Christian should live. I may be free from the bondage of sin, but that doesn't mean I am free to behave any way I want to.

One time in my business, I did something that could have had a negative impact on others. Someone who knew I was a Christian said, "Dick, you are a Christian. I didn't think you would do that." Even though things were not going well for me at the time, I should have controlled my actions.

The ministry of the Spirit goes way beyond what I have shared. As with most of this book, my stories are aimed at living in relationship with Christ.

It has been about fifty years since I attended that Cru seminar. Rare as it is, the teaching I received on the "ministry of the Holy Spirit" has been the greatest discovery of how to make my Christian life work. It is not a religion but a relationship with the living Christ.

Chapter 4

GRACE AND FORGIVENESS

For it is by grace you have been
saved, through faith—
and this not from yourselves, it is the gift of God—
not by works so that no one can boast.
—Ephesians 2:8–9

I grew up in a church that emphasized the importance of doing
good deeds. I understood that if I wanted to go to heaven, it would
be influenced by the extent of my good deeds. There wasn't much
talk about heaven, and it was often considered that good people
would be there and the bad people would be in hell. That provided
a lot of motivation to do good deeds.

Jesus Christ, who talked of loving and serving, was the best
example of doing good things. Another example was my father,
whose reputation was of the highest order. Doing good deeds was
all that was talked about in churches in our town except one. A
small church talked about being "saved," but I didn't understand
what that meant.

They taught that to be saved, you must have your sins forgiven. I thought sinners were essentially bad people who robbed banks, were drug addicts, or committed adultery. They needed to be saved, but I didn't know I needed salvation since I had not done those things, and most people around me thought I was perfect.

I Need to Be Saved

I went to college, where occasionally I attended church, mostly to feel good. Reading a newspaper after church one Sunday, I read about evangelist Billy Graham. His evangelistic crusades were packed, and crowds came forward to be saved, to have their sins forgiven. He used this verse that convicted the people to come forward:

> For all have sinned and fall short of the glory of God and are justified freely by His grace through the redemption that came by Christ Jesus. (Romans 3:23–24)

That verse didn't say "some had sinned." It said "all have sinned." If it is *all*, then that included me. And Jesus was more than a good example. He died for me.

Up to that point, the matter of sin had not been much of a factor with me. My knowledge of the Bible was primarily limited to the psalms talking about how good God is. I only knew about a few things that were considered sins. I thought, *Maybe I am good enough to be saved,* but then I read this verse:

> For whoever keeps the whole law and yet stumbles at just one point is guilty of breaking all of it. (James 2:10)

Little by little, I identified sins I had committed. I thought I was better than most others, but when I understood that with sin, no amount of my good deeds could save me. It was only by the gift of God's grace that I could be saved. Those verses eventually changed the course of my life.

God's grace is hard to comprehend because there still are moments when I don't feel good enough to be saved. As spiritual as the apostle Paul was, there were times when he didn't do what he wanted to do and did what he shouldn't have done. Even he called himself "wretched" and went on to write,

> Who will rescue me from this body of death? Thanks be to God—through Jesus Christ our Lord! (Romans 7:24–25)

Gift of God

It was Christ who paid for my sin, not me. That's grace, God's unmerited favor. I didn't deserve it, but out of His love, He died for me. *You mean I don't have to work for my salvation? I don't have to earn it? It is a free gift from God?* Thoughts ran through my mind. But praise God, I accepted the gift. It has been the most important gift I have ever received.

Did I live a perfect life? No. In his book *The Discipline of Grace,* Jerry Bridges said, "Your worst days are never so bad that you are beyond the reach of God's grace. And your best days are never so good that you are beyond the need of God's grace."[3]

As the word *grace* is used for God's unmerited favor, it also is used for God's Spirit as it works in us whenever we need it. That is why scripture says,

---

[3] Jerry Bridges, *The Discipline of Grace* (Colorado Springs, CO: NAVPRESS, 1994) 18

God opposes the proud but gives grace to the humble. Submit yourselves, then, to God. Resist the devil, and he will flee from you. Come near to God and he will come near to you. (James 4:5–8)

I love these other verses about grace:

Therefore, since we have been justified through faith, we have peace with God through our Lord Jesus Christ, through whom we have gained access by faith into this grace in which we now stand. (Romans 5:1–2)

And if by grace, then it is no longer by works; if it were, grace would no longer be grace. (Romans 11:6)

I am a hypocrite if I receive God's grace and forgiveness and then will not forgive others. The natural tendency in human behavior when offended is to reject the offender. God's standard, however, is to love the offender. Imagine God's reaction when a Christian says, "I will never forgive him."

For if you forgive men when they sin against you, your heavenly Father will also forgive you. But if you do not forgive men their sins, your Father will not forgive your sins. (Matthew 6:14–15)

"They Didn't Do What They Said They Would"

Ginny and I had a history of providing financial support to a Christian ministry. We, along with other donors, were getting older and wondered what would happen to the donor base as people retired or died. As concerned unpaid volunteers, we offered to help increase the donor base.

It would mean selling our house in a place we loved to live and moving 450 miles away.

Before making our final decision, we met with the individual we would work with. We reached an agreement on our job description so we went ahead and sold our house and made plans to move. We looked forward to how we could help the ministry, and I spent many days researching the ministry's work so I could share it with prospective donors.

What a shock when her superior presented a different description of what Ginny and I would be doing! It was a great, big disappointment. We had an understanding, and now instead of presenting the benefits of the ministry, we would just be filling water glasses.

We had already sold our house so we couldn't get it back. What bothered us the most was that, as volunteers, we were the perfect people to ask others to support the ministry. Staff were paid to say good things about the ministry, while we were passionate volunteers who gave of our own money to support the work.

The ministry leader knew about the matter but still didn't do anything about it. As Christians, Ginny and I knew we needed to forgive them. We realized that not forgiving them wasn't hurting them; it was only hurting us to harbor resentment. I realized I was in the wrong for not forgiving them.

> Bear with each other and forgive whatever grievances you may have against one another. (Colossians 3:13)

After three years of bitterness, I was finally ready to forgive. I called the organization's leader and invited him and his wife to have lunch with Ginny and me. The women did their usual small talk while I recounted what had happened and how we wanted to forgive them.

I learned a few things from that experience. The faster we forgive, the sooner relationships can be mended. I offer some words of wisdom.

- Forgiving is a voluntary act. Just forget the issue. It is better to get along than to be angry or bitter. The longer I wait, the angrier I get.
- Christian psychiatrist Dr. Henry Brandt said, "We forget what we ought to remember and remember what we ought to forget."
- Jesus gives us the most powerful suggestion. "Father, forgive them, for they know not what they are doing." (Luke 23:34)

Because of God's grace, others have forgiven me. I can't help but think of this song as I end the chapter:

Grace, grace, God's grace, grace that will pardon and cleanse within;

Grace, grace, God's grace, grace that is greater than all our sin. (Refrain of "Marvelous Grace of Our Loving Lord")

Chapter 5

ABIDING IN CHRIST

Abide in me, and I in you. As the
branch cannot bear fruit by itself,
unless it abides in the vine, neither
can you, unless you abide in me.
I am the vine; you are the branches.
Whoever abides in me and I in him,
he it is that bears much fruit, for apart
from me you can do nothing.
—John 15:4–5 (ESV)

At thirty-two years old, I was the chief executive officer of the smallest of six banks in my city. My primary focus was to grow the bank amid the five larger banks. I would have to put forth considerable effort, which would take a lot of time. When Ginny and I moved to town, we were not Christians but became believers shortly after moving there.

As the bank CEO, my role was to engage in various community activities, often involving early morning meetings, which didn't allow me to spend much time reading my Bible. Frankly, when I did read it, I often couldn't remember what I had just read.

While I had received Christ as my Savior, I had not grown much. Some of my Christian friends talked about having a personal relationship with Christ as if they actually knew Him. I hadn't gotten into the "Praise the Lord, oh, how I love Jesus" crowd, but I did feel like I was missing something. One verse convinced me to finally believe.

> I have come that they may have life and have it to the full. (John 10:10)

If I were to grow, many of my community activities would have to go. I wanted to learn how to experience that fullness. Thirst for the Bible helped me to become more serious about learning what the Bible had to say.

Gradually, when my terms to serve on various boards or community committees came up, I was unavailable. Some people didn't even bother to ask me to serve in various ways because they thought I would be too busy. It was as if Jesus was helping me rearrange my life so my focus could be more on Him.

Prior to this time, reading the Bible was more of an obligation, but now I had a new desire to read it because I wanted to. I felt there had to be more to the Christian life than I was experiencing. My first priority was to have a love relationship with Jesus Christ.

The disciple Luke tells us about the time Jesus was invited to a meal at a Pharisee's house. As customary, Jesus reclined to eat the meal. Learning that Jesus would be there, an uninvited woman entered and went to Him weeping.

Her many tears rolled down her cheeks, falling to His feet. What a display of passion for Jesus as she wiped His feet with her hair and kissed and poured perfume on them! Disturbed, the host could not imagine Jesus accepting this display of emotion from a woman known for her sinful behavior.

Storyteller that Jesus was, He then talked about a moneylender and two people who owed him money. One person owed a very large sum and the other much less. Not typical, the moneylender forgave both debts.

Addressing his host, Jesus posed this question: "Now which of them will love him more?" His answer was "I suppose the one who had the bigger debt forgiven." Jesus commended him, replying that he gave the correct answer (Luke 7:41–43).

Then Jesus challenged the host, pointing out that the host did not offer the customary kiss when He entered the house. The woman kissed His feet. Instead of the host offering water for Jesus to cleanse His dusty feet, the woman emotionally washed His feet with her tears and dried them with her hair, pouring perfume on them. Jesus said to the host,

> Therefore, I tell you, her many sins have been forgiven—for she loved much. But *he who has been forgiven little loves little*. (Luke 7:47)

Self-Reflection

I wondered why I didn't have more of an emotional attachment to Jesus. If I had not had two knee replacements, I think I would have gone to my knees after reading that verse. It was as if I had literally heard Him speak those same words to me: "he who has been forgiven little loves little."

Previously I had not paid much attention to wrongs in my life. I felt that compared to others, I wasn't as bad as they were so there hadn't been much for which I needed to be forgiven. I guess I thought that God graded on the curve.

Not admitting how prideful I could be, I thought God had to provide a way for people to be saved, and I had just taken advantage of it. Hopefully, my good deeds would outweigh my bad deeds.

The moment when I heard the scripture "he who has been forgiven little loves little," I realized how hopeless I was without God's mercy and saving grace. My good deeds amounted to nothing. I did not deserve salvation.

> But when the kindness and love of God our Savior appeared, He saved us, not because of the righteous things we had done, but because of His mercy. (Titus 3:4–5)

It became clear to me why I was not experiencing love for Christ. I lacked genuine appreciation for what He had done for me. Like never before, I pictured the rejected Christ obediently suffering, shedding His blood, and dying on that cross for me. It was as if I was the only one for whom He died.

Whether or not I had truly accepted Christ as Savior before, there was no doubt that I did at that moment.

> And this is the testimony: God has given us eternal life, and this life is in His Son. He who has the Son has life: he who does not have the Son of God does not have life. (1 John 5:11–12)

Now that I was sure of my salvation, how will my relationship with Christ make a difference in my new life in Christ?

Abiding in Christ

I love to do studies of words to enhance my understanding of the Bible. Kenneth Wuest wrote about "abiding" in his *Word Studies in the Greek New Testament.* He refers to Christ in John 15 when Jesus talks about Christians bearing fruit.

> Abiding in Christ refers to a person who maintains an unbroken fellowship with Him. He makes his spiritual home in Christ. There is nothing between himself and his Savior, no sin unjudged and not put away. He depends upon Christ for spiritual life and vigor as the branch is dependent upon the vine. The abiding of Christ in the Christian is His permanent residence in Him and his supplying that Christian with the necessary spiritual energy to produce fruit in his life through the ministry of the Holy Spirit.[4]

As I learned about abiding in Christ, I gained confidence and became more relaxed in my faith. The fruit comes through the vine, which is Christ, and the branch is me. In other words, I don't have to work for righteousness; it comes through what Christ did for me on the cross. I just need to receive it and do something with it.

And even if I make a mistake in a decision, if it is made according to what I consider God's will, He can deal with it. Whether something happened today or next month was fine. I was *ready* for whatever and whenever.

> Readiness for God means that we are ready to do the tiniest little thing or the great big thing. It makes no difference. Be ready for the sudden surprise visit of God. A ready person never needs to get ready. (Oswald Chambers, *My Utmost for His Highest*)[5]

---

[4] Kenneth Wuest, *Word Studies in the Greek New Testament* (Grand Rapids, MI: Wm. B. Eerdmans Publishing Company) 65

[5] Oswald Chambers, *My Utmost for His Highest* (New York, NY: Dodd. Mead & Company, Inc., 1935 Public Domain)

Bearing Fruit

Jesus, soon to go to be with His Father in heaven, told His disciples that "the world must learn that I love the Father and that I do exactly what my Father has commanded me" (John 14:31). He used an illustration that the people would understand: growing grapes.

The point is that we as Christians are meant to be living differently for Christ. If we are known to be Christians, will others recognize it by how we live, talk, and behave? Then Jesus said,

> Remain in me, and I will remain in you. No branch can bear fruit by itself; it must remain in the vine. I am the vine; you are the branches. If a man remains in me and I in him, he will bear much fruit; *apart from me you can do nothing.* (John 15:4–5)

The first time I seriously read John 15:1–17, I was shocked as I read, "Apart from me you can do nothing." I argued with Jesus in my mind, *Don't You know of all the good I do?* It was as if He answered me, "Yes, but for whose glory?"

Maintaining an unbroken fellowship with Christ, making Him my spiritual home, nothing between Him and me, no sin unjudged and not put away, is one way Kenneth Wuest described abiding in Christ.

I am thankful I discovered abiding in Christ. As each day comes around, if I am abiding in Christ, whatever takes place is up to God.

Chapter 6

TRUSTING WHEN LIFE DOESN'T MAKE SENSE

But blessed is the man who trusts in the
Lord, whose confidence is in him.
He will be like a tree planted by the water
that sends out its roots by the stream.
It does not fear when heat comes;
its leaves are always green.
It has no worries in a year of drought
and never fails to bear fruit.
—Jeremiah 17:7–8

Things go better in life if we trust God. I have a history with trusting God, and I must admit that it wasn't always pleasant. Jeremiah's prophecy would have read "a tree planted in a barren desert where it *never* rained," and *no* worries would have been changed too *many* worries. Things had been good in my life, but for a while, it went from bad to worse. I just wanted to give up trying.

What I am leading up to is that even though I had committed my life to Jesus Christ, things were not always as I expected. There were worries, mainly providing for my family. Up to a point, things had gone so well in my Christian life that I hadn't learned much about what it means to trust God when my need was bigger than me.

My Story

What follows next could be called a "saga," a long, detailed account, because I am not the only one who faces situations when trusting God. It is not only difficult but faith challenging.

I was forty years old, president and board chairman of a small bank. Even though I was well respected in my city and satisfied by my board of directors, I told them I would be resigning to accept a position with a Christian organization.

However, arrangements fell through with the organization. Now what should I do? The board offered to have me stay on, but after some serious thought, I felt I should trust God to find me another banking position. My wife never said anything, but inwardly, I knew she thought I was making a big mistake.

When a few months passed and there was no job, it looked like I had made a mistake. *God, why are You so slow? I know You will find me a job, but when? I have mortgage payments to make.* So we sold a bigger house and bought a cheaper one.

I finally did get a job with a small investment management firm, but it would only last six months if either party wanted out. Six months arrived, and they wanted out. I didn't have hurt feelings. I was looking for a job before they hired me, and now I was looking for a job again. One of the partners gave me a book called *Decision Making in the Will of God* by Gary Friesen. He must have figured I would be faced with trusting God to make the right decisions.

Not seeing another available job, I thought I would go into the investment management business on my own and needed to rent an office. A few months passed with no clients and no money to pay office rent. I didn't know whether I was self-employed or unemployed.

One of the most painful times in my saga was waiting on God when I had failed to make two payments on the house. Don't get me wrong; I wasn't just sitting around discouraged. I left the house almost every day looking for a job. I would wake up Monday morning thinking, *This week, I will get a job.* By Thursday, discouragement set back in.

The saga went on. There came a time when I thought, *God, why did You let me quit my banking job? Look at the mess I'm in. Don't You think I should be treated better? With friends like You, who needs enemies?*

Some of the thoughts I had were shameful when things weren't going my way. *I am hurt, hurting, God. Don't You understand?* Finally, I was offered a position at a real estate brokerage firm. Things went well for a time, but the real estate market fell apart. No income. When that happened, I contacted a firm in Atlanta that did financial planning and investment management. They hired me, and it looked like I had a job for the rest of my career.

However, this would not be the case. After three years, I was told I wouldn't be needed any longer. A merger with another firm made me "excess baggage." It was a revolting development at the age of fifty-seven, wondering, *Who wants to hire someone my age?*

As severance pay, I would be paid for six months and access to a job placement firm. I met with the placement manager to sing my woes when it wasn't providing results. How much worse can my situation get? I was hurting so bad that tears came to my eyes.

What Is God Doing?

> Trust in the Lord with all your heart and lean not on your own understanding, in all your ways acknowledge him, and he will make your paths straight. (Proverbs 3:5–6)

I learned much from reading Gary Friesen's book on decision-making, which was given to me when I needed it. Every part of Proverbs 3:5–6 played a part in helping me trust the Lord. He doesn't have to tell us what He is doing, why He is doing it, how long it will take for Him to do it, or what it will mean to me when it is finished.

The six months after I was told that my job would end but I would continue to be paid, I wasn't expected to come into the office. However, I did go in, using the time to learn the successful business strategy of the firm that cost me my job. As I learned, my knowledge and understanding of stock markets grew.

I contacted an internationally known financial publication to see if I could write an article using the little-known knowledge I gained. The lady said, "No, but how about doing a question-and-answer type interview?" That was an even better situation. It took a photographer thirty minutes to take some pictures of me and then forty-five minutes to discuss the material for the article.

Looking back, it was the most valuable seventy-five minutes I spent in my working life.

The publication came out over a weekend, and beginning Monday, the phone rang daily for at least two weeks with readers wanting to talk with me. The response to the article was great, but the client fees were still insufficient to provide for my family's needs.

Waiting on the Lord can be so difficult. Whenever I thought that waiting on God was a waste of time, I would turn to Isaiah 40:31 to gain strength from Him.

But they that wait upon the Lord shall renew their strength, they shall mount up with wings as eagles, they shall run, and not be weary; and they shall walk, and not faint. (Isaiah 40:31)

God's Provision

A friend and his partner had a small investment management firm and felt they wanted my knowledge and experience. I got the job, but there was one condition that they agreed to: spending time with the business was how I would support my family, but serving Christ was how I would seek to carry out God's will.

In other words, I could be in control of my time in the office. Part of my time would be spent researching and serving clients; the balance I could use any way I wanted. I could trust God to both serve Him and still produce a living.

Many of those who read my article became clients and referred others also. Eighteen months after the first article appeared, the publication asked if I would do a second one. More clients came. In the twenty-five years I was associated with the small firm, I never solicited a new prospect to become a client. Yet from referrals, my income grew so that I eventually could care financially for my family.

In taking the job with uncertainties about how much money I would make, I answered what I considered God's call that would take time away from work. *Could I do both without neglecting time in the office?* I never gave up on serving the Lord. As long as I provided what the firm needed to select investments for clients, I was free to do whatever I felt the Lord was leading.

As I tell in the chapter on serving, controlling my time allowed me to make forty trips of ten to fourteen days to Ukraine over twelve years to help a Christian ministry. I could never have taken that much time away from the firm that considered me "excess baggage."

I didn't lose a job; trusting God to provide for my family and me gained me so much more than I could ever have imagined. One of my best resources during this challenging time was Jerry Bridges's book *Trusting God, Even When Life Hurts.* It's a must-read book for anyone struggling with trust.

This old hymn seems to sum it all up:

> Tis so sweet to trust in Jesus, just to take Him at His word.
>
> Just to rest upon His promise; just to know, "Thus saith the Lord.
>
> Jesus, Jesus, how I trust Him! How I've proved Him o're and o're!
>
> Jesus, Jesus, precious Jesus! O for grace to trust Him more!" (Louisa M. R. Stead, 1882)

Chapter 7

BENEFITS TO OBEDIENCE

Whoever has my commands and obeys them,
he is the one who loves me.
He who loves me will be loved by my Father,
and I too will love him and show myself to him.
—John 14:21

Never had I been more motivated to obey the Bible than when I read those words. It was a moment that changed my Christian life. If I wanted to have a more meaningful relationship with Christ and experience more of His love, obedience would be an important factor.

Loving Christ

My dynamic, passionate pastor speaks loud and fast! Sometimes, as he did recently, he repeated himself more than once. I am amid writing this chapter so these words have stayed with me: "Nobody obeys God and in the end regrets it!"

A good friend, Christian psychologist Dr. Henry Brandt, was an expert on obedience. When couples came for counsel, they were often angry at each other, but when he told them what they should do, they didn't want to hear it so they became angry at him. However, the next time they met for counseling, they told him they followed his instructions, which worked, and they wouldn't need any more counseling. That is often the case for us when we're told to obey.

When we think we won't like something, it's like "Taste it; you'll like it." That's how it was many years ago when I didn't eat corn on the cob. My wife said, "Just taste it," which I finally did, and now I may eat two cobs at one sitting!

Generally, I respond better to following "instructions" than "obeying" commands. Dr. Brandt's point is that God's commands are designed to *keep us safe and give us a life of joy and peace.*

Chris Tiegreen, in his devotional book *God with Us,* says essentially the same thing.

> The greatest turning point in a believer's life after salvation is when pursuing God's righteousness changes from an obligation to a delight. Trying to be holy always results in failure after failure. Falling in love with a righteous God results in progress.[6]

In the chapter on abiding, I experienced a defining moment with Christ, but it was just the beginning. God knew I needed to

---

[6] Chris Tiegreen/Walk Thru Ministries, *The One Year Walk with God Devotional: 365 Daily Bible Readings to Transform Your Mind* (Wheaton, IL: Tyndale House Publishers, Inc., 2007) 201

go deeper in my love for Christ. One thing is to know my Bible better, and the other is to obey what it says.

Living a life of obedience does not just happen. We may know that we should be more obedient, but it usually takes some time before deciding when to start.

It is easier said than done.

Whoever Has My Commands and Obeys Them

As I did with the subject of trust, I find that breaking related verses into important points helps my understanding and application.

Jesus's disciples knew Him well from His teaching and examples. He demonstrated His love for them by humbly washing their feet. Obeying Christ's commands means doing as He did. He *showed* them the "full extent of his love" and told them that He had set an example that "you should do as I have done for you" (John 13:1, 15).

The parable of the Good Samaritan showed the hypocrisy among so-called "believers" as they lacked compassion for a seriously injured person, a failure to "love your neighbor as yourself." The "righteous" failed to provide help to a beaten man, whereas another showed compassion by caring for his needs. Jesus said, "Go and do likewise" (Luke 10:25–37).

The disciples knew the "Ten Commandments" given to Moses. Jesus would soon depart to be with His Father, so He wanted the disciples to have a fuller meaning to his commandments. So it was not something new, never commanded, when he said,

> A new command I give you: love one another. As I have loved you, so *you must love* one another. By this all men will know that you are my disciples if you love one another. (John 13:34)

Truth and freedom go together. John 8:31 says, "If you hold to my teaching, you are really my disciples. Then you will know the truth and the truth will set you free."

Obedience was a favorite theme with the apostle John, not only as a key to a vital relationship with the Father and Son (John 14:21–24) but a compelling force of action.

> We know that we have come to know Him if we obey His commands. The man who says, "I know Him," but does not do what He commands is a liar, and the truth is not in him. But if anyone obeys His word, God's love is truly made complete in him. This is how we know we are in Him. Whoever claims to live in Him must walk as Jesus did. (1 John 2:3–6)

Before reading John 14:21, I did what was comfortable. I guess it would be called "selective obedience." There were some things I obeyed and some I didn't. It just depended upon my priorities. I had received Christ, so I was saved, and now I was just doing my best. I guess it could be summed up with these words: *Lord, You can send me anywhere and do whatever You want so long as you give me a nice house, two cars, a social position, and success in my business.*

Those things became less important as I became committed to obeying God's Word. James 1:22 and 25 say,

> Do not merely listen to the word, and so deceive yourselves. Do what it says…But the man who looks intently into the perfect law that gives freedom and continues to do this, not forgetting what he has heard, but doing it—he will be blessed in what he does.

He Is the One Who Loves Me and Shows Himself to Me

Jesus says in John 14:21, "He is the one who loves me. He who loves me will be loved by my Father, and I too will love him."

Have you ever wondered that if you did something wrong, God would not love you anymore? Remember that Christ willingly gave His life so we could be saved, that we may have eternal life.

The apostle John wrote far more about love than any other New Testament writer. Thank God that in 1 John 5:11–12, he reminds us that we have eternal life. Once we have eternal life, it is forever. We may stumble and fall, but Christ is there to pick us up.

And the love of Christ endures forever. Hebrews 13:5, 8 say, "Never will I leave you, never will I forsake you … Jesus Christ is the same yesterday and today and forever."

Whenever I doubted Christ's love for me, I would turn to Romans 8:35. "Who shall separate us from the love of Christ? Shall trouble or hardship or persecution or famine or nakedness or danger or sword?"

And Show Myself to Him

John 14:21 ends with Jesus saying, "And I too will love him and show myself to him." There are many situations where Jesus showed what He is like. At first, I thought Jesus would somehow show Himself to me in some experiential way that I coveted. As things turned out, it would come over time, but first, I needed to know more about Him.

Before I came to Christ, I thought the Bible was full of rules. It told about things in which I had no interest. Attending a teenage youth camp, kids were invited to come forward to dedicate their lives to Christ. In my mind, I thought that if I did that, it meant that I would have to become a missionary. It wasn't for me, but looking back, I didn't know what I was missing.

The more I understood what Jesus said and taught, the more I loved Him and desired to serve Him.

> This is love for God: to obey his commands. And his commands are not burdensome. (1 John 5:3)

I find it interesting that a ministry in India expects new believers to read the Gospels before learning anything else. They needed to know about Jesus before they were expected to follow Him.

> If you love me, you *will* obey what I command. (John 14:15)

It was rather common for Jesus to begin a statement with the word *if* because there was a choice to make. You will obey could mean I must obey, like a command to obey. But it is a choice.

Actually, I found that as I came to love Jesus more, it became my desire to obey and please Him. I found that to be true when I was dating Ginny, who was soon to be my wife. I wanted to please her because when she was happy, I was happy.

The last words of that verse really touched me. I wanted to know Jesus so that I might serve and love Him. Jesus said to His disciples,

> If anyone loves me, he will obey my teaching. My father will love him, and we will come to him and make our home with him. He who does not love me will not obey my teaching. (John 14:23)

A reason so many Christians don't obey Christ is because they don't love Him. They may say they do, but there is no fruit.

Jesus said, "Come, follow me" (Matthew 4:19).

Chapter 8

DOUBTS: BELIEVING ISN'T EASY

Now faith is being sure of what we hope for
and certain of what we do not see.
—Hebrews 11:1

Before and after I received Christ, I had many doubts about
the faith. When my wife received Christ, she had no problem
believing the Bible, especially Christ's words. She said I had more
doubts than all her Christian friends combined.

These are a few of my doubts:

- The Bible can't be true; it's full of fables.
- I doubt that Christ meant all He said.
- Do you really believe God could create the world and
  humans in just six days? There is just too much to believe
  in the Bible.

My doubts were many more than these. Even the disciples
Peter and Thomas are famous for their doubts. Peter needed proof

that Jesus wasn't a ghost walking on water, so he said, "Lord, if it is you, tell me to come to you on the water." Jesus did, but then Peter became afraid and started to sink. I'm sure it was not a rebuke when Jesus said to him, "You of little faith, why do you *doubt?*" (Matthew 14:25–31).

Thomas, sometimes called "doubting Thomas," said, "Unless I see the nail marks in his hands and put my finger where the nails were and put my hands into his side, I will not *believe* it" (John 20:25).

My Doubts Did Not Surprise God

Despite my many doubts, God saved me and gave me a secure place in heaven. Some people use doubts as a basis for not believing, but not me. My wife kept me stocked with great books, and the more I learned from the Bible, most of my questions and doubts were addressed.

I can testify that nothing is so firmly believed as that which has been doubted.

Doubt is looking for light, while unbelief is content with darkness. My doubts did not surprise God; He knew all about them and was not disturbed. Serious about my commitment to Christ, instead of passing over things I doubted or didn't understand, I went to the Bible and other resources to get answers.

Reading good books has helped define my life. When someone mentions a book on a subject I am interested in, I typically buy it. And if I can get by the book's first part and find it interesting, I will read it all. That happened when I read the book *Not God Enough* by J. D. Greear. The title sparked my interest because it suggested that it would be about doubts. I especially identified with this quote:

I have good news for those of you who struggle with doubt: doubt in the Christian life is not only normal; it is divinely orchestrated. Doubt happens when the superficialities of your faith meet the realities of this world. Many of us inherited our faith from our parents, friends, or even our surrounding culture. But God doesn't want second-hand faith. Each of us has to learn to trust God on our own.[7]

Faith and Doubts

Author John Ortberg feels that most people think of faith and doubts as opposites, like oil and water. He makes the point that both faith and doubts are part of life.

Jesus links faith and doubts together with answers to prayer. In talking about prayer and how God would answer it, Jesus said, "I tell you the truth, if you have faith and do not *doubt* ..." (Matthew 21:21).

James asked God for wisdom and expressed a negative consequence of doubting. He said, "But when the person asks, he must believe and not *doubt*, because he who doubts is like a wave of the sea, blown and tossed by the wind" (James 1:6).

In his book of the Bible, Jude sympathizes with doubters, saying,

> But you, dear friends, build yourselves up in your most holy faith and pray in the Holy Spirit. Keep yourselves in God's love as you wait for the mercy of our Lord Jesus Christ to bring you to eternal life. Be merciful to those who *doubt*. (Jude 1:20–22)

---

[7] J. D. Greear: *Not God Enough: Why Your Small God Leads to Big Problems* (Grand Rapids, MI: Zondervan, 2018) 27 and 62

It is not that I encourage people to have doubts, but if we have doubts and are open and honest, committing them to God, He will expose us to answers in due time. Note that I said "open and honest." When I was young in my faith, I would often not express my doubts because I did not want people to think little of my evident lack of faith. Pride kept me from admitting my doubts and finding real answers.

Feed Your Faith; Starve Your Doubts

Wisdom and understanding help resolve our doubts. I didn't know the Bible had so many answers for life. I can be reading my Bible, not especially to resolve any doubts I had, and there right before my eyes is my answer. God wrote the book; He knows the answers. The Bible is His answer book.

> For this reason, since the day we heard about you, we have not stopped praying for you, asking God to fill you with knowledge of his will through all spiritual wisdom and understanding. (Colossians 1:9)

Paul and Timothy prayed in thanksgiving about fellow worker Philemon concerning his faith in Christ and love for others that he might be active in sharing his faith, "so that you will have a full understanding of every good thing we have in Christ" (Philemon 1:4–7).

I learned that when I had a doubt, I shouldn't dwell on it. God's Word is true. Some think the Bible has contradictions, but if they knew and understood it better, they would realize there is no contradiction.

I close with one more quote from J. D. Greear's book *Not God Enough*, "If we make our faith contingent on being able to figure everything out, we will never believe." I highly recommend the book. If I had read it years ago, I wouldn't be writing this chapter. God is big enough to meet us in our challenges and desire to know Him.

Chapter 9

ANXIETY OR PEACE

Do not be anxious about anything,
but in everything, by prayer and petition,
with thanksgiving, present your requests to God.
And the peace of God, which
transcends all understanding,
will guard your hearts and our
minds in Christ Jesus.
—Philippians 4:6–7

There is a wonderful picture of a bird nesting in the crevice of a cliff with waves crashing onto the bank. You would think the bird would pick a safer place, but instead, it is sitting there like nothing is happening. It is at peace.

Who has ever encountered a difficult situation and not lacked peace? It can happen, but it is rare. I remember when I, along with my wife, received a call from our child's school. An illegal substance had been found in her possession. My first thought was selfish. *What will our Christian friends think of us?* The next thought was *How can we change the child?*

Ginny and I talked for a while, and then I had to drive to Chicago on a business trip and be gone for a couple of days. As I was driving, I had a lot of time to think. I was glad to be on an interstate highway because I was thinking more about the problem than the road.

We had tried to keep our child from spending time with kids who were not a good influence but to no avail. Our objections were not welcomed, causing stress in our relationship. It seemed obvious we had little prospect for bringing about the life change that would rule out the attraction to drugs.

We just weren't communicating. Communicating without action is no communication at all. We tried to keep our child on a straight and narrow path, but it just didn't register with her. God doesn't give up. Maybe He could come up with something more effective to bring about change.

Unexpectedly, I recalled a sermon recently given by a visiting pastor. Actually, it was just one verse, but it couldn't have come at a better time, right when I needed it.

> You will keep in perfect peace him whose mind is steadfast because he trusts in you. (Isaiah 26:3)

It was clear why I had had no peace; my mind had been fixed on the problem, not on God. Try as we might, we couldn't change our child's mind, but God could. It was like turning the light on in a dark room. I didn't give the situation another thought until rejoining my wife when I returned.

We were ready to go to sleep when the subject of the misbehavior came up again. My wife asked me how I felt about the situation, and I said I had peace. She didn't share that view and retorted, "Don't you even care?" I replied, "Yes, but I have placed the matter into God's hands; now it's His problem to solve. Let's go to sleep."

From that experience, I became more focused on the subject of peace. If I want peace, I can't allow my mind to be fixed on problems; I need to trust in the greatest Problem-Solver.

Peace Is Found in God

Philippians 4:6–7 offers the best recipe for experiencing perfect peace. Those two verses have given peace to uncounted persons who otherwise would worry, face uncertainty, or face heartaches. I hurt for others as they face trials and disappointments that are difficult to bear and are not experiencing peace.

Living the Christian life in our own efforts doesn't work. Jesus knew that life would be difficult, that we would need a power greater than ourselves, so He gave us the gift of the Holy Spirit who would dwell within us. The Spirit is there to help us experience what we need. How do I know that?

> But the fruit of the Spirit is love, joy, *peace* … (Galatians 5:22–23)

When I decided to take my mind off problems and focus on trusting God, I had peace.

Jesus knows people better than anyone. He said, "I have told you these things so that in me you may have peace. In this world, *you will have trouble.* But take heart! I have overcome the world" (John 16:33).

Today our life is more complicated than in the days of Jesus. There is much to worry and be anxious about. When those things happen, peace is often elusive.

> Who of you by worrying can add a single hour to his life? Do not worry about tomorrow, for tomorrow will worry about itself. Each day has enough trouble of its own. (Matthew 6:27, 34)

We cannot avoid troubles; our circumstances should not dictate how we think and feel. Peace is always available as we focus on God rather than our problems.

Do Not Be Anxious about Anything

I love this quote from Corrie Ten Boom: "Worry does not relieve tomorrow of its stress—it merely empties today of its strength." George Muller said, "The beginning of anxiety is the end of faith, and the beginning of faith is the end of anxiety."

Jesus knew there always would be worry. Before He departed for heaven, He said to His disciples,

> Peace I leave with you: my peace I give you. I do not give to you as the world gives. Do not let your heart be troubled and be not afraid. (John 14:27)

Notice that Jesus said, "Do not let." It wasn't a suggestion; it was a command. The apostle Peter said,

> God opposes the proud but gives grace to the humble. Humble yourselves, therefore, under God's mighty hand, that he might lift you up in due time. Cast all your anxiety on him because he cares for you. (1 Peter 5:7)

By Prayer and Petition

The first thing we should do when we encounter a problem is to go to the Lord in prayer. He already knows our needs. Do we think we can handle our problems on our own?

> You do not have because you do not ask God. When you ask, you do not receive because you ask with the wrong motives. (James 4:2)

There is one way for sure we can trust God in our prayers.

> This is the confidence we have in approaching God: that if we ask anything according to his will, he hears us. And if we know that he hears us—whatever we ask—we know that we have what we asked of him. (1 John 5:14–15)

If we lack answers, God has them.

> If any of you lacks wisdom, he should ask God, who gives generously to all without finding fault, and it will be given to him. But when he asks, he must believe and not doubt because he who doubts is like a wave of the sea, blown and tossed by the wind. (James 1:5–6)

With Thanksgiving

Dr. Bill Bright of Campus Crusade for Christ was the person who opened my mind to the awesome matter of giving thanks to God. It is easy to thank God when things go well, but what about when things go the other way? So often when a tragedy takes place, we are anything but thankful. Dr. Bright prescribed thinking of two verses.

And we know that in all things God works for the good of those who love him. (Romans 8:28)

Be joyful always; pray continually; *give thanks in all circumstances*, for this is God's will for you in Christ Jesus. (1 Thessalonians 5:16–18)

God is sovereign over all things—what is good and what appears to be bad. We are thankful for God's will because He is in control.

And the Peace of God, Which Transcends All Understanding

It is not peace *with* God; it is the peace *of* God. Once we have accepted Christ, we are a child of His. Nothing, no nothing, is impossible with Him. Our personal peace *of God* can change from hour to hour, but it doesn't have to be that way.

Sometimes friends may say, "I don't understand how they can be so peaceful in the midst of the circumstances."

I don't understand all things that happen in my life while they are happening. I just need to realize that God is in control. He doesn't match His wisdom with anyone because He will always come out the winner.

Oh, the depth of the wisdom and knowledge of God! How unsearchable his judgments and his paths beyond tracing out! Who has known the mind of the Lord? (Romans 11:33–34)

Will Guard Your Heart and Mind

What does it mean to guard your heart? Proverbs 4:23 says, "Above all else guard your heart, for it is the wellspring of life."

By being wise and discerning in our lives, we don't stray from what is true. Our *minds* need to be protected so we may not be unknowingly deceived.

> Do not love the world or anything in the world. If anyone loves the world, the love of the Father is not in him. For everything in the world—the cravings of sinful man, the lust of his eyes and the boasting of what he has and does—comes not from the Father but from the world. The world and its desires pass away, but the man who does the will of God lives forever. (1 John 2:15–17)

To me, peace is like an anchor. It keeps me secure, even amid storms. When I could be anxious, peace holds me steady. I feel like I am in God's hands, sheltering me from what would harm me. Jesus said,

> But seek first his kingdom and his righteousness, and all these things will be given to you as well. Therefore, do not worry about tomorrow, for tomorrow will worry about itself. Each day has enough trouble of its own. (Matthew 6:33–34)

Chapter 10

FAITH AND HOPE

Faith in God has been the backbone of my life. However, He was not a part of my life until I was thirty-two. I knew some things about God and Christ, but trusting in Christ for my salvation took faith. Looking back, it was the greatest decision I ever made. For by grace, I had been saved through faith.

God's Spirit assures us that a Christian can develop an enduring character with three wonderful things. Along with love (which is another chapter), they are faith and hope. All three have one common aspect: they remain and abide until the dawn of eternity. The reason they remain is simple to see.

- They are grounded in God.
- They are centered in Christ.
- They are established in the Spirit.

Eternal Truths

These are eternal truths that endure forever. Faith is the soul looking *upward* to God. Hope looks *forward* to the future. In writing to the Thessalonians, Paul tells them what he remembers about them: their *work produced by faith* and *their endurance inspired by hope* in the Lord Jesus Christ.

Paul praised people for how they lived and what they did. Even when Paul had to rebuke someone, it wasn't to discourage them but to uplift them. We should feed the good things we see in people's lives and starve the bad things. The more we encourage others about the good they do, the less bad we will see.

As Paul praised believers, he thanked God that their faith was growing more and more. If the inspiration to work is because we recognize it is God's will, we will do it joyfully as we seek to please and honor Him through our works.

This story about bricklayers who were building a cathedral makes my point. One man said, "I am laying bricks because they are paying me to do so," while another said, "I am building a building." Then a third man who loved God said, "I am building a cathedral for God!" Wherever there is *true faith*, it will work and work gladly.

The last thing Paul mentioned was their *endurance inspired by hope.* Wherever there is a well-grounded faith, hope will endure. A man can endure anything as long as he has hope, for then he has something to look forward to.

Some people think that poverty is a lack of money, but I think it's a lack of hope. I gave poverty another meaning when I taught the Bible at a women's homeless shelter. These women had children, but the fathers couldn't be found. They had little hope of caring financially for their children. Poverty is when people give up hope and quit trying to find a job. If a person has hope, there is a job out there to be found.

Faith

> Because you have seen me, you have believed; blessed are
> those who have not seen and yet believed. (John 20:29)

It took some time, accompanied by a measure of doubts, for me
to accept Christ as my Savior. Once I realized God loved and
forgave me, I became more open to trusting Christ. Without
faith, there is no Christianity. Faith believes in what God has
said, and it is sure of what we hope for and certain of what we
do not see.

In some parts of our world, enemies of our faith face Christians
with the choice "deny Christ or death." We see on TV their
choice of death. Thank God we live in a country faced only with
devoting our lives to live for Him.

Now I pray for Him to live in me that I might live His will.
Paul said, "I have been crucified with Christ and I no longer live,
but Christ lives in me. The life I live in the body, I live by faith in
the Son of God" (Galatians 2:20).

When I turned my life over to Christ, His Spirit in me gave
me the desire to seek God's will. It has been said that there is no
safer place than to be in the center of God's will—dead to self,
alive to Christ, and seeking God's will.

Hope

> Therefore, since we have been justified through faith,
> we have peace with God through our Lord Jesus Christ,
> through whom we have gained access by faith into this
> grace in which we now stand. And we rejoice in the *hope*
> of the glory of God. (Romans 5:1–2)

Hope is faith looking forward to something with joyous anticipation, for I know it will happen and I'm looking forward to it.

> For everything that was written in the past was written to teach us, so that through endurance and the encouragement of the Scriptures we might have hope. (Romans 15:4)

Hope dispels the darkness of the world around us. It is the assurance that enables us to bear any difficulty and enables us to believe the best in any situation. Yet all of this depends upon us drawing upon the very life of God that flows to us in a constant stream from Christ.

Joni Eareckson Tada turned pain and suffering into hope. As a teenager, she incurred a back injury that would be permanent. Crippled, she had lost the use of her arms, hands, and legs for life. I once read that her response to this tragic situation was this:

> The best we can hope for in this life is a knothole peek at the shining realities ahead. Yet a glimpse is enough. It's enough to convince our hearts that whatever sufferings and sorrows currently assail us are not worthy of comparison to that which awaits over the horizon.

That gives me hope to carry on in this life. With God, there is help and a hope, a place of safety even though we may be hurt.

> We must come to Him daily, even moment by moment, and He will give us the hope we need to live in this world with all its evils and wrongs. (Phillip Keller)

Let me mention two portions of verses from Hebrews 10:22–23.

- Let us draw near to God with a sincere heart in full assurance of *faith*.
- Let us hold unswervingly to the *hope* we profess, for he who promised is faithful.

These two aspects of the Christian's faith and hope are also summed up in 1 John 3:2–3.

> Dear friends, now we are children of God, and what we will be has not been made known. But we know that when He appears, we shall be like him, for we shall see him as he is. Everyone who has this hope in him purifies himself, just as He is pure. (1 John 3:2–3)

The last part of this verse essentially said it was up to me to *purify myself.* I have been saved by faith in Christ; now it was up to me to make Christ the Lord, the master of my life. As I did, and over time, life in Him became everything I could hope for. I wouldn't trade it for anything this world has to offer.

Chapter 11

LOVE ONE ANOTHER

***

And now these three remain: faith, hope and love.
But the greatest of these is love.
—1 Corinthians 13:13

***

According to my Bible concordance, the word *love* is used in the Bible more than five hundred times. More than half are in the Old Testament and are often repeated and refer to God. Without an actual count on how the term *love* is used in the New Testament, it is safe to say that most of the time, love is aimed at "one another."

Love isn't just an important aspect of the Christian life. In 1 Corinthians 13:7, Paul said it "always protects, always trusts, always hopes, and always perseveres." The Bible doesn't just deal with the subject one or two times; *love* appears in every New Testament book except Acts. Paul often referred to faith, hope, and love. As important as faith and hope are to the Christian life, nothing compares in importance to love.

Addressing the believing Colossians, Paul told them to act like new people in Christ. With Christian virtues, they should bear with each other and forgive whatever grievances they had against each other. He said, "And over all these virtues put on love, which binds them together in perfect unity" (Colossians 3:14).

Love in Action

As I prepared to write this chapter on love, several situations came to mind. I chose three of them. The stories are true, but the names, other than my wife, are made up.

> Dear children, let us not love with words or tongue but with actions and in truth. This then is how we know that we belong to the truth. (1 John 3:18–19)

Jane was a cashier at the drugstore I frequented. With a face full of ugly warts, she was not one to compete in a Miss America contest. Since she was at least fifty years old, I assumed nothing could be done to remove them.

Our society places so much emphasis on beauty. Her condition would likely be an obstacle to someone choosing to marry her; however, I discovered she was married and had children. Kids can be hurtful among themselves by making fun of people. I could imagine some kids saying about Jane, "You know, that lady with all those ugly warts."

The more I came to the drugstore, the more Jane's appearance bothered me. *How would I feel if people stared at me like I was doing with her?* The words of Jesus came to me as I had learned them as a child. "Do to others as you would have them do to you" (Luke 6:31).

The love of Christ has no conditions; we are all created in the image of God. I was convicted to change my attitude and was pleased to do so. God's ways are always the right ways.

Things changed. I became drawn to Jane. Instead of avoiding her, I was happy to have her wait on me so I could greet her with a big smile. I asked about her family and thanked her for waiting on me. It was great to experience the transformation by following Christ's example.

I Need Help

Joe visited our church so I called him to set up a time to get acquainted and answer any questions he might have. We met at his apartment a week later. There was the typical time of small talk about the church's various ministries, especially about our singles group.

Instead of responding with interest, he seemed apprehensive. If I had known him better, I might have probed to determine if something bothered him. As I was getting ready to leave, he was not ready for me to go.

Our conversation had been cordial, and he appeared comfortable talking with me, but now he opened up more about his life. We had been talking about the church, and now the conversation turned to him. He wanted—no, he desperately needed—some help. It was an emotional moment.

Joe had been involved in the gay lifestyle for years and had a partner. With a pained look on his face, he told me that he had accepted Christ six months earlier, and it did not go over well with his partner. Rather than experience delight in this new relationship, Joe's life was in turmoil.

Before I continue, I need to say that what I am sharing are Joe's words. My position on this serious issue is to quote these words from the Bible:

Whoever does not love does not know God, because God is love. This is how God showed his love among us: He sent his one and only Son into the world that we might live through Him. This is love: not that we loved God, but that he loved us and sent his Son as an atoning sacrifice for our sins. (1 John 4:8–10)

As the word of Joe's conversion spread to his lifestyle friends, they couldn't imagine him choosing Jesus Christ over them. Those who had been his friends now became unfriendly; instead of well-wishing, there was bitterness. As he told it, weird, scary things took place. He had one close lady friend who encouraged him, but his situation was becoming desperate as he looked for help. There was no one he could turn to.

I wanted to help Joe but had little knowledge about the gay lifestyle. I couldn't just leave him with the typical "Best wishes." Lost for words but wanting to help, I said, "Joe, I do have experience in knowing *how to love someone*. Here's the deal: I would be pleased to meet with you weekly over breakfast if you are interested. That takes a lot of time, but if it could help you, I am willing to give it."

At the beginning of our time together, I sought to help him realize that his need for a Savior and mine were the same. It's one sinner talking with another sinner. We became bonded friends. A true love relationship is two imperfect people refusing to give up on each other. I was committed to helping him; he was committed to learning from me.

There were times when both of us shed tears. When that happened, we would leave the restaurant to go to my car to continue our conversation. This went on for two years.

Through my help and others in my church, Joe grew in his faith. It is evident that his life with Christ has endured. In time, he married and fathered three children. To help others find new life in Christ, he has written a book about his story.

Love One Another

Ginny and I met and dated when in college. We were together as much as we could be. I never imagined I would be so fortunate to marry someone like her. She was popular, talented, and smarter than me. How could I ask for anyone better than her? One would think she is perfect.

I was a bit surprised when I began seeing things differently after marriage. Before we married, I thought she didn't know how to cook, but she was a good cook. However, I recognized some bad faults that began to bother me, things that I felt needed to be changed. But her response was "That's the way I have always been."

It bothered me as I focused more on her faults than her good qualities. We both had become Christians, and to follow Christ called for changes in the way we thought and behaved. There was never a serious problem in our marriage. However, I knew things could and should be better.

At first, I thought I could make Ginny change, but it takes time to change long-standing habits. Then I realized it would work better if I worked on my own faults first so that I could be an example to her. What would it look like if I did that?

The apostle Paul taught about virtues: faith, hope, and love, and the greatest of these is love! Here is what he said about love:

> Love is patient, love is kind. It does not envy, it does not boast, it is not proud. It is not rude, it is not self-seeking, it is not easily angered, it keeps no record of wrongs. Love does not delight in evil but rejoices with the truth.

It always protects, always trusts, always hopes, always perseveres. (1 Corinthians 13:4–7)

Wow! That is asking for a lot! But I could see that if we both followed these verses, what a glorious marriage we could have. But I needed to focus myself on me.

- I will be patient and try to do better.
- I will be kind and want to help you.
- I will stop bringing up things from the past.
- I will be understanding and not get angry so easily.

But what about Ginny and her faults? If I am going to be able to love her more, I would have to love her *in spite of* her faults. And if she doesn't change, I still have to love her *in spite of* her faults.

So I tried it, and it worked. When I focused more on Ginny's qualities and less on her faults, it wasn't her problem but mine.

I guess what I want to say in each of these situations is the following:

- Love for Jane is *doing to others* as you would have them do to you.
- Love is *giving* two years helping Joe.
- Love *in spite of* teaches me how to love *more*.

Chapter 12

ENCOURAGEMENT

We have different gifts, according to
the grace given to each of us.
If is it to encourage, then give encouragement.
—Romans 12:6, 8

This chapter was probably the most satisfying to write in this whole book. My heart is really aimed at relating personally with Christians about their Christian life, especially younger people. It's a real blessing to see them get excited about their faith.

Every time Ginny and I moved from one town to another, which was fairly often, I looked forward to organizing a small group in our church. I called them "growth groups." It was a great way to meet new people, but my goal has been to help them grow in their faith.

I didn't allow the groups to get large in number, nor did I allow anyone to monopolize the time. The idea is to create an atmosphere where people feel comfortable openly engaging in group discussions.

Wonderful things happen when people are more open about sharing their lives. In that atmosphere, there is a bond with each other that can last for years. I know this is true because that bond formed with Ginny and me and six of the eight others from a small group I led thirtysomething years before. I was the person leading the group while the others were in their twenties and young in their faith. An airline pilot named Matt asked questions on top of questions. I couldn't believe how little he knew about the Bible.

Fast-forward thirty years.

Matt's wife invited Ginny and me to meet them for dinner at a favorite restaurant. We did that often, so it was nothing special. Matt opened the door for Ginny and me to the shout of "Surprise! Happy birthday, Ginny!"

What a joyous time we had reminiscing about things of the past. We laughed about some of the questions Matt asked in the past. But the most important thing was that each of them was living fruitful Christian lives, for which they thanked us for our Christian example and encouraging them to grow.

If it hadn't been for that small group and being encouraged to grow, who knows if they would even be members of a church today?

His Name Is Barnabas

Every church ought to have at least one Barnabas in it, and it would be even better if there were many of them. The first time Barnabas was mentioned in the book of Acts, his given name was Joseph. It appears he was called Barnabas (Son of Encouragement) because he sold a field he owned, brought the money, and put it at the apostles' feet (Acts 4:36).

Imagine what churches would be like if people thought

more of giving and helping those in need rather than taking for themselves. Barnabas did this at a time when many early Christians suffered financially. Believers voluntarily agreed to not claim what they owned solely for themselves but would share with others. Barnabas did that, not that he had to but because he wanted to.

Another man and wife sold a piece of property but decided to keep part of the proceeds for their own use, which was their right. However, when questioned by the apostles, the man lied and said he brought all the money. The man was told, "You have not lied to men but to God" (Acts 5:1–4).

God knows our heart; is it about me or about God and others?

If you look at synonyms for the word *encouragement,* there are many. Here are just a few: *comfort, console,* and *exhort.*

Comfort

What really fulfills me as a Christian is being to encourage people when they suffer various kinds of trouble. I learned how important it was as others encouraged me.

In the midst of an adversity I wrote about elsewhere in this book, I needed a job. I thought, *How am I going to make the next mortgage payment?* Jim, a wealthy Christian brother, knew of my situation, but I never asked him for help. Day after day, I faced my problems until the day when I opened an envelope in the mail from Jim. Much to my surprise, I found a check for $5,000!

What a relief it was—just in time to make a mortgage payment and more. Thank You, Jesus, and thank You, Jim! He must have read these verses:

> Praise be to the God and Father of our Lord Jesus Christ, the Father of compassion and the God of all comfort, who

comforts us in all our troubles so that we can comfort those in any trouble with the comfort we ourselves have received from God. (2 Corinthians 1:3–4)

It used to be that people considered the Bible to be important to hang on to their life in thick and thin situations. Psalm 23 would rank among the highest.

The Lord is my shepherd, I shall not want. I will fear no evil, for you (the Lord) are with me; your rod and your staff, they *comfort* me. (Psalm 23:4)

Console

It usually doesn't do any good to sympathize with people. Sympathy says, "I am so sorry you have the problem." To empathize is a different matter. Empathy says, "I know what it is like; soon it will pass."

When Jesus told the disciples He would leave them to be with the Father in heaven, they didn't know what they would do without Him. So He said,

Let not your heart be troubled: ye believe in God, believe in me. In my Father's house are many mansions: if it were not so, I would have told you. I go to prepare a place for you. (John 14:1–2 KJB)

Jesus felt the need to console the disciples about His leaving, saying,

I have told you these things, so that in me you may have peace. In this world, you will have trouble. But take heart! I have overcome the world. (John 16:33)

If Jesus consoled His disciples, we need to console and encourage others also.

Exhort

Of all the gifts of the Spirit, I think *exhortation* and *comfort* fit me the best. I love it because it is so involved with others. Good or bad, I have something to say that will help others.

Exhortation simply means *encouragement.* I try to be understanding and cordial, but above all, I want to see people grow in their faith. To be a fruitful Christian, a person needs to grow in their faith and help others do likewise. It is gratifying to see a new or weak Christian be happy about the growth in their faith.

Once I observed a young man seriously paying attention to a speaker. He took notes while others looked like they were listening but had their minds elsewhere. I thought, *This is a person who appears to be ripe to disciple.*

After the event, I spoke to him about meeting for breakfast. He didn't question why; he probably thought it was just social to get to know each other. We talked about many things, including our faith.

When it was time to part company, I disclosed, "Jimmy, we seem to have the same interest in growing in our faith. How about if we meet weekly?" He agreed. He was twenty-nine and a Christian for just a few years. On the other hand, I was eighty-seven and a believer for fifty-one years. He didn't know much about the Bible, while I know my Bible better than he does. I can be a teacher; he can be a learner.

We started by reading the Bible together; he read five verses, and then I did the same. Moving rather quickly, we would move from one Bible book to the next. Time did its work, and soon we were digging deeply, studying God's Word. When he didn't understand something, I would answer or explain the meaning.

This went on for months, and one day he said, "Dick, I can't meet with you any longer." I asked him why he felt that way and was excited to hear his response. "I want to do for a new Christian as you have been doing with me." He wanted to find another person to exhort.

At my advanced age, I have retired from my moneymaking work, but I don't read any place in the Bible that Christians retire from the work of the gospel. I just have more time to make disciples. I want to go out strong.

Chapter 13

JOY IN SERVING

Whatever you do, work at it with all your heart,
as working for the Lord, not for men,
since you know that you will receive
an inheritance from the Lord as a reward.
It is the Lord Christ you are serving.
—Colossians 3:23–24

The subtitle of this book ends with *Serve the Lord*. It appears last not because serving is not important but because we first know and love the Lord before we *desire* to serve Him.

To serve takes a desire to help; it is thinking about the needs of others and to serve others in love.

When I see a need, by serving I do something about it, as if it is the will of God for me. Serving is an unselfish act done for others, with which I have great satisfaction. I decided earlier in my life that I wanted to go out strong; I would serve the Lord as long as I was physically able.

Putting it all together, "I am *available*. God, use me as You wish. It is not *where* I serve but *how* I serve. I am qualified for some things but not everything, so I will go where I feel You are calling me."

Setting the Stage

My first foreign mission trip was to Russia with a team of American Christians who engaged Russian schoolteachers. I was motivated to go when I heard an awesome report from a close friend who had just returned from such a mission. It sounded like something I wanted to do, so I signed up for a future trip.

The fall of communism meant freedom of religion. Christian ministries flocked to Russia to spread the gospel, which was greatly needed. Among various opportunities, a group of American Christian ministry leaders met with the head of the Russian Department of Education, who complained about the low state of morals plaguing Russia. Eager to see change, she accepted a proposal to receive teams of American Christians to acquaint Russian schoolteachers with material on Christian ethics and morality. These Bible-based materials would then be taught to millions of Russian children.

Then an opportunity came up for me to join a team of fifty-three people. Our purpose was to meet for four days with groups of ten to twelve teachers in two separate cities. In both places were curiosity and acceptance. It was a glorious experience.

Since our team would scatter once we arrived home, we met to share experiences before our flight would leave for home. Several shared their concern that the Russians had so little whereas we had so much. We had Bibles and other Christian materials in great quantities whereas they had none. No wonder ethics and morality suffered. One lady quoted the following verse:

From everyone who has been given much, much will be demanded; and from the one who has been entrusted with much, much more will be asked. (Luke 12:48)

That verse spoke to my heart. *I have so much. What about me?* I expected to retire from my daily work in four years. *What will I do with my time then? What about spending more time serving God?*

God is full of adventure, but He doesn't always reveal all His plans for our lives. It's up to Him to choose who, what, where, and when to serve.

Once God decides something needs to be done, it is never a matter of *if*. The issue is usually *who?* Who will step forward, embrace the vision and move ahead by *faith?* The beginning of a great work begins as God works in our hearts. (Keith Boggs, *Real Momentum*)

Opportunity Knocks in Ukraine

Our pastor had recently been with a group of American Christians in Ukraine who told him about a ministry that had just formed to teach pastors and equip church leaders. The information didn't fall on deaf ears. Returning home, our pastor shared some information with the missions committee chairman, who remembered my conversation about serving in the former Soviet Union. He contacted me about going to Ukraine.

We went, saw, were impressed, and gave a good report to our church. I thought that would be the end of the matter, but it wasn't. It was just the beginning of a wonderful relationship.

The time was ripe because the freedom to own and teach the Bible was now available. How or what to teach led to organizing BEE Ukraine (Bible Education by Extension) to equip much-needed pastors and church leaders. This wasn't a small-scale situation as the need was nationwide. Since they didn't have Bibles or Bible teaching, there was a great response for the training BEE offered. The ministry spread from under one thousand to several thousand, which meant more books and leaders were needed.

It would take a lot of money, but the leaders felt God would provide so they quit their jobs with no assured income. A one-time gift provided enough money to buy books for the first few courses, but since the leaders had no other income, they used the proceeds from book sales to live on. Then they didn't have money to buy more books. Desperate, worried, and needing to pay for food and health services since communism had ended, they considered disbanding the ministry.

I was getting faxes (no email yet) telling me of the financial needs. What really got to me was that they had no money to pay for the medical needs of their sick children. Under communism, they had free medical care, but now they had to pay for it. *Where could they find the money?*

If Not Me, Who Then?

Who am I? It was just me. If I offered to help solve the need for financial assistance and was unsuccessful, the suffering would be even worse. To my knowledge, I was the only American aware of the problem.

If I see a need, I try to serve. BEE was making an impact, so it would be a shame if it had to be shut down. The hunger for the Bible was extensive, and the desire to form new churches was spreading. The hunger for the Bible was extensive, and the desire to form new churches was spreading.

Some months earlier, I was asked to provide lectures at a large conference of BEE leaders and students. I thought about my theme. Under communism, ordinary people were denied higher education because they were Christians, and most had never been a leader of anything. They needed confidence in believing in themselves. If they didn't lead, who would?

Considering all this, I chose the title of a recent book I had read, *If Not Me, Who Then?* by Cabell Brand, to be my theme. Here I was, trying to decide if I should offer to raise much-needed funding for BEE. I thought, *If I don't do it, who would?*

Pondering my decision to help, those words haunted me: "If Not Me, Who Then?" God convicted me to let the BEE leaders know I would do my best to help raise needed funding. It now was no longer a question of "Should I?" It became a question of "How can I?" I had never sought donors, let alone for a ministry in a faraway, foreign place.

It was now time to ask for help. I said, "God, I am available. You multiplied a few fishes and loaves to feed thousands. I'll trust You to use my availability to accomplish this purpose."

Taking that step of faith was a defining moment. I didn't know if I could be successful, but I knew whom I would be serving. Many American churches became financial partners through the assistance of my awesome pastor, Johnny Hunt. A large American Christian foundation responded to a simple letter from me to meet numerous needs.

I did my part by being *available*. God did His part in *multiplying* my efforts.

Somewhere I have heard this saying: "*I will do my best; my Father will do the rest.*"

It Will Soon Be Over

After nearly twelve years involving forty trips to Ukraine, it became time for me to end my assistance to BEE. My aging body didn't like overnight flights. Mutual deep love and appreciation developed, but now it was time to say goodbye. They had depended upon me, and now it would be up to them to entirely rely on God.

It wasn't easy to tell the BEE council, on which I had served, that I would discontinue my active involvement in eighteen months. I didn't provide anything but time, energy, and personal money, which was a joy to give. God was just using me as a channel to direct financial help to BEE. Nevertheless, the event focused on me, what I had done for them, and our love for each other. *What would express the deep feelings of my heart toward them?*

Paul had a wonderful relationship with the Thessalonians. The people meant so much to him. I decided to share two of my favorite verses with them. To make the verses personal, I exchanged the words "our" and "we" with "my" and "I" and read to them:

> For what is my hope, my joy, or the crown in which I will glory in the presence of our Lord Jesus when He comes? Is it not you? Indeed, you are my glory and joy. (1 Thessalonians 2:19–20)

Serving is not an obligation; it is a blessing. I didn't have to serve in Ukraine; it might have been considered a sacrifice to many. God doesn't see it in that way, and neither do I.

EPILOGUE

I hope that, having read this book, you will have a greater appreciation for God's Word that leads you to the abundant life that Christ offers. He is more than a great example. In fact, He Himself said,

> I am the way and the truth and the life. No one comes to the Father except through me. If you really knew me, you would know my father as well. (John 14:6)

Christ Is Supreme!

It was important for me to acknowledge that God was supreme, not only in creation but in my life.

> He is the image of the invisible God, the firstborn (born before all creation) over all creation. For by him all things were created: things in heaven and on earth, visible and invisible, whether thrones or powers or rulers or authorities, all things were created by him and for him ... For God was pleased to have all his fulness dwell

in him, and though him to reconcile to himself all things, whether things on earth or things in heaven, by making peace through his blood, shed on the cross. (Colossians 1:15–16, 19–20)

Jesus Resides in Our Hearts

As I saw God as supreme and myself as so much less, I desired a relationship with Him. The apostle Paul speaks of Jesus Christ.

For this reason, I kneel before the Father, from whom his whole family in heaven and on earth derives its name. I pray that out of his glorious riches He may strengthen you with power through his Spirit in your inner being, so that Christ may dwell in your hearts through faith. And I pray that you, being rooted and established in love, may have power, together with all the saints, to grasp how wide and long and high and deep is the love of Christ, and to know this love that surpasses knowledge—that you may be filled to the measure of all the fulness of God. (Ephesians 3:14–19)

Wise versus Foolish

It became clear that the wise are not those who reject the shed blood of Jesus for salvation; it is those who accept it. I needed to accept not only the supremacy of God but also the forgiveness of sin that reconciles me to Him.

For the message of the cross is foolishness to those who are perishing, but to us who are being saved, it is the power of God. For it is written: "I will destroy the wisdom of the wise; the intelligence of the intelligent I will frustrate." Where is the philosopher of this age? Has not God made foolish the wisdom of the world? For since in the wisdom of God the world through its wisdom did not know Him, God was pleased through the foolishness of what was preached to save those who believe. (1 Corinthians 1:18–25)

What Are Your priorities?

As a result, I was overwhelmed with gratitude, thanking God for His mercy and desiring to serve Him.

> Therefore, I urge you, brothers, in view of God's mercy, to offer your bodies as living sacrifices, holy and pleasing to God—this is your spiritual act of worship. Do not conform any longer to the pattern of this world but be transformed by the renewing of your mind. Then you will be able to test and approve what God's will is—His good, pleasing and perfect will. (Romans 12:1–2)

I challenge you to think through your own defining moments that have brought you closer to God or away from God. After reading this book, do you have another defining moment? How do you want to live your life?

If you would like to contact me, I'm at RichWalsman@gmail.com or mail me at Dick Walsman, 141 Sweetbriar Farm Road, Woodstock, GA 30188

ACKNOWLEDGMENTS

Dr. Tim Warner – He exceeded my expectations as an ex-missionary and started my walk toward Jesus Christ.

John Bruehl – I wanted him as a customer; he wanted my soul for Jesus. Without him as my early mentor, you would not be reading this book.

France Schaeffer – As a new believer, he taught me "true spirituality."

Oswald Chambers – His *My Utmost for His Highest* devotional was too deep for my young faith, but once I got serious, it was my spiritual food.

Dr. Bill Bright – There is no higher calling or greater privilege known to man than being involved in helping fulfill the Great Commission.

Dr. Henry Brandt – I learned much about the Holy Spirit as he told me, "Your walk with God does not depend on people, places, things, or events."

Jerry Bridges, author – When I thought God had abandoned me, *Trusting in God Even When Life Hurts* was an anchor to my faith.

Dr. John Edmund Haggai – He came into my life when I

was having doubts if I could complete a contractual obligation and assured me with his famous quote. "Attempt something so impossible that unless God is in it, it is doomed to fail." And I did.

Pastor Johnny Hunt – His passion for winning souls for heaven was infectious. He once said he wanted only one word on his gravestone: "Others." He has influenced so many people for good.

And a special acknowledgment goes to Maggie Bruehl, an author herself. She offered to help as needed, and while I thought it would just involve providing some limited advice, she coached this first-time writer almost every week. She was as inspired as I was to see the message of this book touch the lives of as many people as possible. Her patience and encouragement led me to the finish line.

Printed in the United States
by Baker & Taylor Publisher Services